DETONATE I

We fall in love countless times in one life time.
Ony one love can ignite and heal the soul.
That's a forever love!

FAITH KC

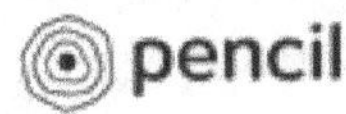

ISBN 978-93-5667-335-9
© FAITH KC 2022
Published in India 2022 by Pencil

Contributors:
Co-Author: Ruth KC

A brand of
One Point Six Technologies Pvt. Ltd.
123, Building J2, Shram Seva Premises,
Wadala Truck Terminal, Wadala (E)
Mumbai 400037, Maharashtra, INDIA
E connect@thepencilapp.com
W www.thepencilapp.com

DISCLAIMER: *The opinions expressed in this book are those of the authors and do not purport to reflect the views of the Publisher.*

Author biography

Writing is a hobby i've had since i was 12. I've realized that the more you pen down your stories, your brain sharpens faster. When you slow down or take a break; it get's rusty. To all the readers, i hope this awakens the soul.

CONTENTS

Foreword

I was never a woman to settle for less.

i always wanted more! Winning wasn't an option, it was my game. i loved it. I loved the feeling of being at the top, The view up there fascinated my entire being and the spectacle left me in a daze.
And like the night, i wished for the stars.The brightness of them dazzled every fiber of my nerves. I would do anything to get up there, I would not trade that feeling for anything in the world until him.

Preface

Dedicated to Jacob Atwine.

You saved my life in a million little ways you will never understand. One day, I hope the stars will rewrite history for the better.

To the beautiful you!

6am found me on a bus to Niamey central business centre south of Olobre. I needed to be on time to save myself the drama of sitting in the queue for the interview. Nonetheless, I loved keeping time. I would be doomed if my brother got to know I was late for a job that had left me dancing on needles with excitement. It was only a 45minute drive leaving me with approxiamtely 15minutes to have breakfast and 10 extra minutes to check my dressing or use the lavatory and seven minutes to have my name called into the "interrogation room.

Two more stops and my turn would reach to alight. My hands fondled the small rough paper in the jacket for the millionth time in half an hour. Tucking in the coluna braids behind my ears, i took one last btreath and told myself i got this.

I had no time to have breakfast and instead used the time to take prepare my rehearsed speech which I modified every second. I was the second early birder next to a gentleman who looked like he had just hit his thirties. His face had a more relaxed eloquence and elegance of a sophiscated gent with an aura, aloof as his gaze.

Ten minutes later, the receptionist directed him to the office on the first floor as she told him, "they are ready for you now." Buttoning his suit jacket, he picked his bag and strode with a laziness that spoke of power and exquiteness. It was not until now that i registered the cologne that swiflt wafted to my nostrils and heightened my senses. The feeling indescribable. His face scrunched up in one scrutinizing gaze when he realised i had somehow stopped in my tracks and was openly staring at the charcoal black suit in awe left his eyes filled with amusement. It was obvious he knew the kind of effect he always gave off and fed on the expressions that came off the people that came off those he met.

And once again, we were all led into the conference hall at exactly 9am to do a paper that just teased my brain endless. The questions were a blow to my IQ but something i could handle. Later at 11am, we were made to face the board sitting at the panel before they handed us our results.
One of the interviewees was excited as she narrated to the rest of us how her uncle was part of the board and how surely she would get the position. For the rest of us, like me; I had to rely on my grades and brains to pull this off.

"Tomiola Linda please take the stand."That name jolted me out of the seat and sent my palms dripping with sweat in nanoseconds. Straightening my dress, I brisky walked to the front in long quick strides.

"You're miss Tomilola?"A masculine voice sounded through the microphone and following the voice, I was met with the coldest pair of eyes.

"Yes, please. That's my name."

""Alright then. You graduated from Griffin University with a first class upper in nursing right?"His brow arched up as he scanned me from head to toe and i nodded in affirmation.

Änd you also did a short course in speech therapy, attended a summer camp for teenage counselling and did your research in HIV prevalence among the youth. This is just another set of a well wrtten CV. Apart from your good grades, what else can you bring to the table?"

"Sir, please if i may speak freely." He gestured a go head with a thumbs up.

"Yes i do have good grades on paper and they aren't enough to get me this job.
I am a mother and part of my parent description is to ensure i provide financial security to my son. I also know that this is a privileged hospital that handles the upper class in the city and the country. I am a multitasker and efficient especially in the pesiatric department. I just find myself naturally bonding with them. I really want this job.
  Yes.
This is an opportunity ideal to actually develop my career.
And i belive that nursing is skill, it's patience. it's individualized and i'm not claiming I know everything but i love learning. I enjoy working with a team that's driven with passion to put others first. This hospital offers me the

stand; to get acquinted with a learning culture due to it's massive specialised clinics. I love winning, not just as a person; but as a group Am still holding on to the same, so i become better at providing services better.."

"Well then, how would you mange a patient with DKA ?"

Tomilola wowed the head nurse with her descriptive answers as she started explaining. Not only was her figures of speech enriching, she could see that the woman had every streak of leadership in her.

The panel later offered lunch to the interviewees. Tomilola took the opportunity to ring her brother and ask how Jason was doing. She loved her son to death that she always kept tabs on him.It surprised her how her prepared speech had quickly disappeared from her mind the moment she stood up.On hanging up, she realized her fate hung in the balance. She needed this job from all angles but she wasn't going to force fate this time around.

In the late afternoon, she was notified by the head nurse that she would not be getting the position. Her heart braced for what came hext after this. She had been at wits ends until that ad in the newpaper four days ago. For Jason's sake, she needed money. Sister Faridah later gave her a contact and advised her to call immediately as she was sure Tomilola would be getting a job at the said location she had scribbled on paper. The latter embraced her tightly before walking out of the building.Probably Angella had finally got the spot since her uncle had made the process easier.

"Moma."

That sound made her heart skip each time and she founde herself kneeeling and bundling up her joy in merriment. He was the source of her strength in all this.

"Jace. My sweet little pwimkleball."

The tickles sent both of them rolling on the floor with high pitched giggles.until Divine walked in from the kitchen.

"Tomi!"

He just held her tightly when he saw the look on her face. He could see how she was trying to hold back the down pour from her eyes. They glistened the more and he knew he had to let her know he had her back. Doing his excellent rubs with his knuckles on her back, she took in a deep breath before she mouthed a thank you.

"Ï prepared your favorite you know; it's time to eat,"

Divine tucked Jason in bed after his bath as Tomi made a phone call. Her mood couldn't have gone any worse as the caller was unavailable at the moment.

Sleep remained the only option to soothe her weary mind. The moment she closed the door behind her, her legs wobbled to the ground effortlessly as she broke into a sob. This was getting the best of her. She needed a solution real quick and fast to do away with her problems at once.Where would she get a solution for all the bills?

She had to pay rent, water, electricty, Jason's medical checkup that was pending. Least to her problems, she knew she could get the money she wanted if she just agreed to Eric's proposal.

Just one night and her problems would end but her brain scolded her for even thinking about a solution as despicable as that good for nothing man. There would be only one man after that night six years ago. Her body curled into a ball and she passed the night there on the cold cement.

"Don't break Tomilola. Dawn is breaking soon."

She would have thought it to be an angel in her dream had it not been for the worried expression on Ritah's face.

"Ritah?"

"Linda!"

"Ritah, Linda oh my gosh!"

They both chorused as they wrapped each other. It had been close to six months from the last time they had seen each other. Ritah found herself holding on a little too tightly than she had anticipated. She felt guilty for not being there for her friend when she needed her the most.

"I've organized a trip to Kenya. i also got you a new passport while you had your beauty sleep."

She teased while Jason walked in dressed in his uniform while Divine packed the lunch box.

"I'm sorry sweetheart i couldn't prepare you for school."

She tossed off the covers and reached for her son.

"Oh moma. You need to sleep so you look more beautiful. Plus, auntie Ritah said a change of environment would surely make you happier. Also, I know you love me very much so I will be the best son in the world for you moma, okay."

A small tear snaked down her right cheek as she took in all that Jason said. Why did he have to be very sweet like the man that fathered him? The four of them all converged in a group hug around Tomi. She knew they saw throough her facade of bravery and her stunt of always being strong. Even at this point, she still couldn't let anyone in completely.

New beginnings

Kithumi bus park.

Ritah, Linda and Gerald a mutual friend of theirs made way to the taxi. Fourteen seater old cracky Hiance model that scooted gas bad enough to make the intestines grumble. They were to spend three days in the small town just East of Nairobi. A lot of trees, so many dispersed homes and murram roads. Just an off the grid place where she could clear her head.

The three of them took the back seats since their destination would be the last. Reading the text on her phone, Ritah smiled inwardly at the surprise she had for her friend. She hoped this would be timely fresh air that brought healing in their hearts. Funny how no one had informed their parents that they had travelled out of the country.

Everything had turned out easier since a national ID or passport was the only thing needed at the boarder. The road scenery lushed with all green. People grew a lot of fruits and vegetables. The waters far beyond filled her with calm anticipation about dipping in cold waves and let them carry her into their depth. Drown her sorrow in the waters and come forth refreshed. Ritah retold her first visit to this place. She was met with a beautiful river and falls, a history about how everyone would find the man they loved if they made a wish at the waterfall with a coin. The story sounded like a myth to Linda and she couldn't help but smile wryly at the superstition.

She was never one to believe in such! When the taxi pulled to a stop near the village market, it brought back memories of home. The fabrics that the people wore were purely African. How she loved the ebony, the mahogany tints and soft patterns of the thread in the material. The vastness of the place wowed her as the guide picked them up and directed them to the four wheel parked across the road.

Young man with soft dreads and interesting pleasing King's English. Tomi stole a few glances at him before she got caught and had to bow her head low. If she had a pink glow it would have been plastered all over her face. He watched her alluring amber skin glow brightly under the rays of the orange sunset. She was a beauty. Ritah had not made any justice while describing her to him.

Fifteen minute drive, the jitney parked.

Kimani camp site.

Drawing her phone out of her black jean pocket, she switched on her mobile data and made a video call to Divine. She needed to make sure Jason was okay. Her heart started racing when he informed her that her son had asked him about his father. He had returned from school in a sour mood after a coupple of children had bullied him.

She worried for how he was doing. It was unlike Jason to inquire about "Him."

Was her past finally catching up to haunt her? Were the mistakes she thought she had dearly paid for become an unsettled debt she would never clear? Her thoughts jolted to a stop when Samuel the guide interrupted her reverie. She almost tripped on her own legs if not for the timely savior of the moment who caught her midway before she could meet the ground.

I'm sorry. Linda whispered and roughly pulled onto her bag tugging it close to her body while walking to the reception. Ritah was quick to throw her the bunch of keys and direct her to their place of residence. Just down the corridor, room 4 next to the wood cottages. An old fashioned traditional yet classic with wood art, pieces of paintings and linen curtains.

Huge and oblong with one painting of a pot and another of a field all green with happy people smiling, probably a family. White with large window frames of wood. A cozy bed just single for her body to feel the silkness and a large mirror on the wall. Her lips curved upwards as she walked into the bathroom and screamed at the tub and the scented candles. This was kindness she did not exactly know how to repay. She couldn't believe Ritah had paid for all this. The masseur called to make an appointment for 9am the next morning.

Clad in a summer polka dress, Ritah sashayed down to the cool blue water that soothed her thoughts. Her mind kept racing to the group chats she had read. Roman would be walking down the aisle in less than two months if she did not do something. There was a lot from the past that meede to be straightened. Linda still loved him. She knew that for sure because she had not seen another man after him.

Oh how Linda gave her heart to a man who would never reciprocate her affection! She lamented inwardly at the saddening thought.

Was it love or just stupidity or even an obsession? She wondered as she reminisced how she had met Samuel. The attraction was mutual. Their energy matched. No one had to sacrifice to make anything work.

Looking back at Linda; her heart shattered in a million glass pieces. She needed to do something. If Gatheca had helped her get her life back on track, then he would do it for Linda. She just needed the right time to hit the jackpot and try baiting her into agreeing to the plan. The former would never agree to what she had to say in her right senses but she had to try. Tomilola Linda had eerything within her to get everything she ever wanted. Just the right amount of strings and power and all would be alright.

Linda hummed a chorus before bunning her hair up in a pony tail and dipping her body in the covers. Divine was right. This place had a lot of magic. Her spirit ignited, she picked up her journal and scribbled a few paragraphs with a smiling face. Perhaps, she needed to start living again.

Not just for her dreams and Jason, for everything that she yearned for.

Crossing her hand on the chest, she listened to the child in her screaming to bring the walls down. It was as though the solution that had been lurking around had made known to her that it was time.

"Narrator."

Troy sat at the round table applauding his best friend on finally getting serious with Michelle and asking her to marry him. It had been a surprise when Jonathan had showed up at his door step earlier that morning and asked him if he wasn't rushing on settling down. He had just completed his internship in medicine and surgery. Though he knew that he would have waited to place a ring band, he was exctited when she had said yes to being exclusive.

She had secured a scholarship to Toronto for her master's degree early the following year. Losing her wasn't an option and the only way to tie her down was to make her his other half. Oh how loving Michelle was peaceful.His body tinged just thinking about her. What they had was peaceful.

What was left was to sit down the parents and communicate a date for the traditional marriage and then plan for a church wedding. Expenses were not an issue to worry about as he had a fat job that paid handsomely.

He was even the head of department at the hospital he worked and part of the staff managing committee. He wasn't going to wait until he was a millionaire to marry. He would dive all in and build a forever with this woman.

Michelle Agonza. Toffee skin complexion, beautiful smile, flawless dentine and big brains. Petite and charmingly stunning. Everything about her melted him. She was just perfect!

"Salum."

"Cheers."

The click of glasses and merriment echoed in the gardens of Elle resort.

"How I love you Mich."He planted a kiss on her neck and her face turned coffee with giddiness. She closed her eyes savoring the feeling of his lips on her skin. Jonathan Roman Atwine. She would be a Mrs.Atwine. That man! Danm! How was she lucky to meet someone so perefect as him!

Tilting her head, she tugged slowly on his shirt and drew him in a passionate kiss. A hunger pent up just for their bodies. That was enough to send bolts to the right reions. She left him breathless before pulling away and musing how she had that effect on him.

"You know what happens after here future Mrs.Atwine."

Husky was his voice. The burning sensation that had taken control of his body threatened to explode any minute. He loved that his life was finally settling calmly without any dramatic escapades. Holding tightly around her middle muscles, he pulled her closer till her frame was directly in contact with his. She could feel the fire she had ignited and giggled with a knowing smile when they exchanged glances.

Better days had indeed arrived!

New beginnings II

"Dante. It's nice to see you again."

"Öh! My daughter, How life is smiling down on you. Karibu my mtoto."

"Asante baba." Ritah led the rest of them to the living room of the house. Linda squirmed countlessly under the scrutinizing gaze of the old man. Gerald seemed to notice how uncomfortable she was and gently squeezed her hand while offering a small smile.

The man served them roasted sweet bananas and milk tea and other herb spices.

Under other circumstances, she would have had the bananas because she liked them. This time around, it seemed her hands hand glued down on her laps and froze there.

"Tomilola."

The way he said her name jerked her attention towards him. Her brows furrowed in confusion at how he would know her name. Ritah wasn't helping with the situation as she seemed to enjoy the show. She sipped cozily on the tea and chewed lusciously the bananas on the saucer. On noting the confusion plastered on her face, Dante smiled widely as a father would do.

"Don't worry Tomilola. Whatever you wish for is within your grasp. As for your name, that's icing to the cake. This is a small town where everybody knows everyone so it's not hard to know the guests who come by. Also, I own the campsite where you will be staying this weekend."

Tomi's tensed body seemed to relax with the explanation. Her hands finally drew the cup to her lips. It had cinamon and vanilla aroma wafting to her nostrils that she cloed her eyes on sipping and let the warmth of it slide down to her throat. It was more that she expected.

"Asante, Mr. Dante. This is really good."

" Sawa. That was to help with the nerves. I should say you're a beauty in person. Ritah did no justice in her descriptions."

Her brows arched amusingly. She listened with her mouth agape in incredulity.

Ritah smirked brushing off the comment and shrugged.

He smiled before exiting to the next room and Ritah followed him. They spoke in hushed tones. Ritah stashed out two notes of a fifty dollar bill before gently thanking the man. Only if this could work out.

Ritah later explained that Mr. Dante had sort of psychic powers and could predict anything in the future. He even had a page, Predictor with almost one hundred fifty thousand followere that had ever tried his services. She urged Tomi if there was anything she wanted to ask, to give it a try.
Gerald excited stood up and left to confirm what the former had said. It wouldn't be a bad thing to try the guy out.

He returned his face contorted with childish excitement and thanked Ritah with a bear hug. The revelation had taken him off guard and threw him into the abyss. He had ditched a woman that loved him to death and could have risked her life for him. She had been destined to be his soulmate. Only if he had known that she was only being difficult for the sake of her family, he would have exercised a little more patience with her.

He was deeply repentant for causing her pain. Maureen! He had to win her back. From what the old man had said, he would have more stability than he had in his life if she were by his side. His career was taking off mediocally and Dante had given him the exact connections he needed.

He joined Ritah in beseeching Linda to see what would happen. He believed they had all met in this small town for a reason. If this is the change that they needed, he would gladly receive it. The latter hesistant said she would try probably another time. It wasn't until Ritah promised to tell her why she had left six months ago, on that rainy stormy night that Linda found her footing. It had been a scary experience that had left a scar. If Ritah was willing to share the details, then she would give this a try.

Skeptical, Tomilola stood up just and walked to the room which Ritah had quoted as the consultation arena. She wanted to prove to her friend just how such people wgo are soothsayers play with people's psychology just to extort money from them. She would never believe in scam like this.

On entering, she noticed lit candles in a circle and Dante seated in the centre. He beckoned her to come in and join him in the circle. She smiled knowing how this was the exact stunt she had been thinking. Why can't these people do away without candles?

He replied to her thoughts that candles signified light. Protection. And above all, it illuminated the soul. Not only did others use pentagon shapes while connecting to a higher power, he preferred the circle. Sitting in that yoga postion with both hands settling comfortably in sync. Her father though younger than him would never sit in this position without complaining about his knees and back.

His voice echoed in her mind. "This age is surely killing me. Look at how i've lost my touch, my skin is now wrinkled. Oh baba! I"m too oldo. People will call me a mzee now. Tomi, don't forget me oh. This man here your baba." A memory dearly treasured. She felt nostalgic.

Her body sunk sitting in the same position staring at the man whose eyes were closed. From her judgement, he was nothing paranormal. No glowing or light shining from his body. He was just like anyother human being meditating. The surrounding had no eerieness.

"Child, pumua. Tomilola Linda, daughter of Mahange Mwasa, you're the first born in that familia. Please close your eyes, and i let Moyo wako. Mutima. Align with the universe." His voice bellowed as the room started spinning and he held her hands in his.

"Wh--- whhta what is happening?" She felt light headed and her body sway with wind blowing until she could see herself sitting by the road on top of the hill, the exact one she used to hike with Roman.

"I know you feel cheated why you'd love someone who doesn't love you back. You must be in pain that you cannot tell your son, Jason who he's baba is. Yote yalianza ulipomwambia rafiki yako about your love life. What you did not know, this same friend of yours had eyes on the same man. Thta's when your problems started. I know you have asked yourself why this is all happening to you and you question God countlessly. It's all coming to an end. The moment you walked in here, I could see the loneliness in your eyes. You find consolation in your son becuase he looks exactly as the man who fathered him.

You closed the door to any man who has tried to knock on the door of your heart because there's a part of you that loves Jonathan Roman Atwine. You only dream of starting a family with him. That is why when you found out you were with child, though cast out from the family by your father; You chose the baby over your parents."

"Seems like Ritah did a goood job telling you all about my secrets. Danm it she couldn't keep her mouth shut." She thought bitterly while staring at the muddy road and recalling how he had held her out here in the cold for the first time. How his hands had wrapped her coyly. At the time, they were friends. She was struggling with her family to get them to see why they needed to let her have a mind of her own which hadn't been possible.

This had the second memory with the man she had grown fond of and loved deeply up to now. What despondence!

"Ritah said nothing about you to me. I know your deepest fear is losing your family. Your deepest secret is that on 12th July of the same year you concieved, you made an oath with a friend of yours that your souls would be tied together and forever. Later that same month, on 27th, Roman asked to grant you three wishes. Among them, you told him you wanted him in your life forever. What you did not know, the oath you had made jokingly with your other friend; was a blood oath. You only realized it too late when they started blackmailing you into doing their bidding." He restrained himself from mentioning the name like it was a bad omen. Had a deadly streak to it. He spurted venomously the last bit his body quivering tormentingly.

Warm liquid started slipping down flooding her cheeks and blurring her vision. The things we do without arming ourselves for the consequences.

Dante stopped talking at once when the door flung open. He knew she was losing consciousness. That he could tell from the whitening of her face. From afar Roman's face appeared in a blur before everything around her darkened painfully.

Wishes

Ritah called Samuel the next morning to find out where he was. He asked her to meet him at the local butcher's shop. On getting there, he was no where in sight.

"Small baba where are you?" She asked playfully but the man had not seen the indulgement in the unadorned joke.

"What's that supposed to mean? I don't like you calling me small baba. How can the whole me be just small abi. I just love being called Samuel not baba. Baba small. Small baba?" He was pouting so adoringly that she had to stop her body from roaring with hearty laughter.

"Do all babies behave like you baba mtoto?" She innocently repeated and watched his face contort in disgust. He had promised to leave her tongue-tied the next time she pulled a stunt like that.

"Well it's not like am a baby. It just happened that after me my mother couldn't bring herself to bear another child. So that doesn't make me a mtoto or a spoilt kid. Though come here." He said with a mischevous tint in his eyes.

He drew her before flunging her up in the air. She screamed when he showed reluctance in holding her down.

Nearly down and he firmly grounded her.

An hour later, they returned from the local market.

Tomi opened her eyes groggily with the pounding in her head. Hushed voices and people surrounding her bed. Ritah was quick to give her a cup of locally brewed tea to help with the headache. The two had been taken by surprise when Dante called for help to carry her to the guest room.

Gerald couldn't hold back the questioning directed towards the old man wondering what could have happened for her to end up in a comatose state. He still lit yellow candles around the bed where she had been placed and put a cold wrap on her forehead. He later explained to them that he had let Tomi confront the truth at once so that she could finally move on to the future.
Ritah couldn't believe that the two had spent the entire day inside the room. It was dusk already and Samuel had come to pick them up.

Gerald volunteered to bring Tomi's phone on her request.

Samuel caressed Ritah as they stood by the bedside watching over her. She knew after this trip, everything would align for Tomi as she tucked the stray strands of her hair behind the ears.

Dante returned with a smile on his face and told everyone to excuse them for a bit as he had something private to communicate with Tomi.

He informed her how the scholarship she had applied for while still in school would find its way to her when she returned home. Her relationship with her parents would improve drastically on a rather disastrous event. The financial doors she had been hoping for for so long had finally opened when he took time to pray and break the curse after she had passed out.

The man she would be spending the rest of her life with would meet her on the day of Jason's birthday. That was less than a month from now. Lastly, her father would be reaching out to make amends before the year ended.

He spoke so softly that she would take in all he was saying without missing out on anything. He later poured some scented oil on her forehead and massaged it into her temples.

"You need to get some sleep, tomorrow is your big day."

His image faded slowly. By the time Gerald returned with the mobile, she was heavily sound asleep. He placed the device by the bedside table and listened in to what Ritah was telling Samuel before he excused himself to go and rest.

At 10pm, Ritah found herself snuggling deeply into Samuel as they snoozed. She grinned satisfactorily when he's strong arm tightened the hold on her waist.

Divine sat dreamily by the window in the shared bedroom with Jason as he watched lazily at what was going on in the city. He had had a panic attack again when Jason couldn't breathe properly. The boy had trekked from school while it was raining because his mates couldn't stop tormenting him about his mother. He had wailed when he had been told that his father had left him because he was so ugly and his mother was with him out of pity.

The unbearable pain that knifed his tender heart had made a run to where he would find safety, home. By the time he made it to the door step, he was wheezing. Had it not been for the kind neighbor who had offered him a change of togs, he would have had a severe asthma attack that God for bid would have claimed his life.

Watching the innocent sweet face deep in slumber, he was entirely grateful to his stars for being merciful. He would have suffered Tomi's wrath if anything happened to her snores. He now perfectly understood why she always referred to his soft snores as music. He drew the curtains back in position and further tucked in the covers before he took to his bed.

Roman lightly stirred in his sleep when her image showed up.

This had happened twice from the time he had slept. For heavensake it was six years now, he had moved on. None the less, not once had he loved her beyond friendly affection. She was a beautiful woman yes; Just not for him. She wasn't his type.She had destroyed his life and that of many others. Goodness Lord the woman was a schemer. She lied about everything to the dot.

So why the hell would her image pop up in his dreams. That smiling dimpled face of hers!

His mood faul, he shoved the covers off his body angrily and walked into the living room. Looking at the framed photograph of Michelle and him reminded him that he's life was back on track and better now. He would have children with her and even give her his surname. He couldn't see anyother woman most deserving as she. Not to say the least, his parents had approved of his choice.

Until the night of the wedding, would he show her his world. He warmed the water and made coffee before picking his lap top to finish the weekly report for the department.
As he clicked the log off button, it was already close to midnight. He's eyes heavy, he removed the spectacles and walked to the bedroom. He watched Michelle sleep for a while before joining her into bed and pulling her into him.

His head hit the covers and a smile spread across his face.

Demons of the past

"Life is not fair, it never was. Isn't now and never will be. But it becomes what you make it."

Dante said those words as he comforted Tomi early morning as they left. He had given her solutions to what she had asked and even provided solace when she sought his advice. She had admitted to have had the most peaceful sleep in the longest time. She buried herself in his embrace before thanking him again. The old man wrapped her and told her to drop by sometime in the future as he would be waiting.

Her demons were silenced. Powerless and held no chain. She felt a live. She felt serendipity. The surge of positivity was a new thing she fully embraced. They were to take a ride to Werosi city and spend the last day of the visit there.

She found herself excited when the vehicle pulled back in the parking lot. She nearly jumped out when Samuel announced that there was a mall they could shop from. She grabbed her African print bag and kicked the door open. This was surely a sigth to behold.

Teslim Megamarket. She took the flight of stairs hurriedly after sighting a jewellery store. Divine loved hair pins and she would be getting him some. Ritah bought a knitted sweater, brown leather craft shoes and a hat. Samuel returned with ice cream cones which they shared. As they walked to the second floor, Gerald pulled Tomi to the lottery lounge and the rest had to follow. None of them had ever gambled. Though a waste of time and money as Linda had called it, he bid her try her luck and see.

She was supposed to pick three lucky numbers. The draw happened every ten minutes. He removed a five hundred kenya shilling note and handed it to her to try. Exchanging glances with everyone there, she proceeded to the counter. Deposited the money and filled a form with her numbers. The woman at the reception handed her a printed card with her ID number and the didgits she had picked.

They all stood waiting impatiently for the count down. The moment the ninth minute hit the clock, Tomi grabbed Gerald's chocolate and took a large bite to ease her tension. Her body felt intoxicated and enruptured for no good reason. Her brows dampened and so did her palms. It felt like enternity. Ritah placed her hand on her shoulders and the former aghast hit the ground.

The tenth minute clocked and the ring of the central machine echoed in the store.

ID number BRT 456799, lucky numbers 711. you have own Kenya shillings, three million six hundred thousand five hundred. Tomilola Linda. Ritah smiled knowingly and enfolded her before the rest joined in. It's like they all knew about this from the way they were acting. The energy with which they enveloped her was completely amazing. She had never felt so good in her life like she felt now.

Dante's voive echoed in her head.

"Your financial door have opened, grasp the door."

He had said those words to her the previous night. Tears streamed freely as she held on a little too tightly onto the three of them. She held Ritah like a life raft and the latter gave her a meaningful nod.

"You're indeed a sister Ritah Layola Katamba or heaven sent. For everything."

They bundled each other up before leading her to the counter. The money was directly transferred to her account on her request in an hour.

The journey to this place had changed a lot of things for her. Converting the amount she had won was almost ninety million in her country's currency. She had Jason's gift wrapped for his birthday and stashed it neatly into the suitcase. They would be taking an afternoon flight than the bus. She was more that thrilled to surprise Jason with her early return.

Ritah informed Gerald and Tomi that she would be staying for a couple more days to spend time with Samuel. They had a wedding to plan before the year ended and her mood elated everyone except for Dante who of course had a knowing look. She handed over a well wrapped navy box to Tomi as a gift to Jason. Samuel ignited the van with all of them seated and they rolled into the parking lot an hour later.

They stood there chatting this and that when the boarding cam announced their flight. On exhanging pleasant goodbyes, the two left to the boarding station.

Hannah Mwasa, rushed to the emergency room. She could barely breathe when Divine had rung earlier with devastating news that her grandson had been hositalized following a "minor accident." The small boy had a venturi mask covering his oxygen. The sudden surge of frustrated affection when at the sight of him and compassion were borderless that she couldn't get a grip of whatever was happening.

Her husband who had been with her held her hands gently and warmly. He knew his relationship with his daughter was strained. He was a man who barely knew the word affection. If not for the soft spoken woman he had married, he would never have known that love would buckle his heart with chains of despair. It had been seven long years from the time he had physically set his eyes on her.

He requested a transfer of the boy to a private room. He'd forgotten to comourflage his looks when he realized the pointed gazes in his direction. They had probably caught wind that he was a big shot from the security detail that had taken stand around the area. In the room, he sat Divine down and asked him to relay what had actually happened.

The man intimidated by the scrutinizing gaze of the former narrated the details hurriedly as he searched for a way out of the situation. Mr. Mwasa knew that his daughter loved and treated this man like her own flesh. He was the only friend who had proved the test of time. He knew his wife took a liking for this young man from the time they were five. She was so fond of him from the time Tomi had intoduced him way back in freshman year. He was just a little off the ages until she had bluntatly annouced that she was with child. At first he had thought that the bastard had poked in territory where he wasn't welcome.

In reality, it had been this young man who had stood by his daughter when she had decided to walk away from the family. He had not disowned her. He had been so mad that night. He couldn't take it that his heiress had been disflowered by a man she could not even have. They had everything. Money, people at their disposal. Connections in the government yet she had chose to walk away from all this and bed a so called Roman.

His thoughts would have worked around the entanglement if only the lad held something for her. To his dismay, she was the one who gave everything wholeheartedly. At some point he found his eyes stained with guilt that he had scolded her continuously and called her a shame to the family. She had denied him access to the man who had got her heavy and even relocated to a different city. It was only this man that had stood by her side all this while when he cut off communication and contact. This was a punishment she had to learn the hard way.

There was a time he had given her the option of getting rid of the child only for her to refuse vehemently. She swore to wage war with anyone who did not support her decision of keeping the baby. Frustrated to the brim, he had walked away keeping his distance as a disappointed father.

Now he understood why his wife was so fond of Divine. He had been the only support system that Tomi had had in her time of need when he had turned his back on her.

The nurse informed the doctor that Jason had regained consciouness on her round to check the progress. Divine requested the old man to goc check on his nephew and his heart bled. He worried if this man had at one time taken a liking for his daughter. Before he could nod in affiramative: "I'm sorry."

Divine's face twisted before meeting the exgen's eyes.

"Haaaa. Sir, what was that? Just to make sure i had correctly." He asked cautiosly just in case he had not heard correctly.

"I am sorry Divine. To you, Tomi and my grandson. I should have handled the situation better may be this would have never happened"

Meekly, he found his hand reaching out his hand to the young lad for support. His wife was sobbing quietly a feeling alien when he felt a tight pinch on the inside. He preferred when her laughter though annoying sometimes reminded him that this more than a politically arranged marriage their parents had orchestrated.

"General sir just to make sure you won't cut my balls out. Will you buy me lunch? I'm farmished." Divine feigned childishly while whinning and Mwasa laughed. This man was all sorts of things. He was going to take his time appreciating the people in his life after this.

They had hardly left for the hospital canteen to grab a bite when Divine's phone flashed.

Sunset whispers

Tomilola's anxiety shot up when she rummaged through the house and no one was present. Where was everyone. She had returned to rewrite the mess she had caused in the past.

She needed to call a truce with her parents for the sake of her son. The rest, she would leave to God. Malloy had been kind enough to drive her home. She had bid them farewell and rushed into the gate so thrilled to give them a surprise of a lifetime. She was a day early from the planned time.

"Divine! Hello. Why is no body home?"

"Wait, aren't you supposed to be back until tomorrow?"

His voice cracked. In a small tone he whispered that they were at the hospital because Jason had been involved into something he couldn't say. Tomi nearly tripped on her feet as she rushed to hail a ride.

Goodness Lord! Her son was in danger while she was away.

Pressuring the rider to speed up, they made it in half an hour. She took the stairs two at a time after paying her fare. She was directed to the private ward first sloor room 14. The sickening gut feeling that was growing left her tangled in wits of fury. She should have been there for her son. She was such a bad mother to leave when she was needed the most.

The door swung open and she stumbled in. Her body did not register the pain from the bruises on her knees until she stood up aided. She prayed the floor would swallow her up. The hold on her hand though firm was astonishingly gentle. The same grip that had helped cross the road in childhood. The same one she had missed. She became a pail of emotions. Her eyes glistened at the sight of her parents. Her mother rushed and enveloped her in a tight embrace. Mwasa was tied on what to do.

Divine held onto Jason's hand as they exchanged glances.

""Tomi. My beautiful girl. You've grown into a wonderful woman." She held on tightly again before releasing her and beckoning her husband to draw nigh.

"Dad. Da--d." She walked up to him. He helped her up before she could drop to her knees. He had surely lost the touched he had always joked about. His head was now a mass of grey. He's sight strained that he would now add spectacles. The wrinkles on his forehead more prominent. The time away from home had taken a toll on him like it had on her. She couldn't stop sobbing and for a moment she forgot about the person hospitalized.

He took her out of the room and led her to the parking lot. He needed to have an open conversation with her. God knew how long he had before he succumbed to the dead. The best odd he had to bet was make peace with life and with the people who mattered. After all, dogs though loyal would never inherit his wealth. His blood would.

They spent three hours rewritting and sorting through their differences. On returning, Hannah was chatting with the doctor how Jason was fairing. He joked how her grandson was the exact carbon copy of a friend of his. They laughed about it when he made for the door.

Tomilola and her father. He would recognize that face from anywhere. Damn! What a night of wonders. He nodded in acknowledgement before hurriedly walking out. He couldn't stay. She had barely noticed is presence as she was so engrossed with the conversation she was now having with her parents or so he assumed.

Had something happened between Roman and Tomilola? The boy's age on the patient's chart was six. Calculating backwards, he couldn't be more correct. It dated to around the time they were together. His thoughts just couldn't wrap around the idea that the two could have done something. The baby resembled him to the dot. From the button shape and high nose bridge, to the same deep set eyes and pouty lips. Tomilola's nubian nose was out of question. They even had the same slanting M shaped luscious and glossy lips. The revelation was beyond him.

He was stealthily going to do a cheek swab to find out later.

"Dr. Ahumuza." His thoughts were interrupted by the incharge nurse who needed his input in the intensive care unit.

10:00pm

Hannah volunteered to spend the night in the hospital much to Jason's dismay. He had wanted his mother to pass the night too. What a mummy's boy! Divine had chipped me scoldingly when he started sulking. The happy grandmother had to pull her majestic stories to calm him down. She had to let her daughter rest from the long trip she had had. Mwasa even requested that she spend the night home instead of their apartment in the outskirts of the city.

It had been miraculous that they had been around town for the security convention that week when the call came in. Divine had mistakenly rung them instead of his boss. He had wanted to ask an off when the principal had phoned him that they were in thr regional hospital. Hannah had jolted him out of sleep saying something bad had happened to their daughter. Like a wake up call, he had picked the keys from the livingroom and the rest was history.

Jason requested her to narrate any stories from his mother's childhood which she so gladly did.

Tomilola had always had a mind of her own. She knew that from the moment she birthed that this girl, was every definition of defiling orders. She had ideally taken after her father. A reason why had to always butt heads.

The chirping of the birds woke the princess out of bed. Her hand rubbed her eyes snuggly as she yawned softly. Martha and Loraine jumped into bed besides her each taking a side. They had been so afraid the previous night when their father had warned them against noisily gossiping with Tomilola around. He kept checking up on her later in the night an old habit he had. The two sisters couldn't wait to bond with their elder. Such a pity how she had cut off almost all communication and left them for the occasional hi's and hey's that held no intimacy.

Having her around was everything. They yelled as they tugged on the sheets. Mwasa smiled as he sipped coffee while watching the morning break news. His happiness would fully return once Tomi agreed to stick with family. That was all he could ask for in this lifetime. The screaming from the bedroom followed by high pitched giggles as they fought on who looked better, who was their sister's favorite was a sight to behold. Tomi felt drained that she had to yell to quiten two adults who were supposedly at the same university. She knew how her father prided himself in providing the best of the most prestigious.

She was the simpleton who preferred doing things the hard way on her own. That was always a tug of war when it came to territories. An hour later. they all drove into the hospital's parking lot. Jason's discharge was complete and only a signature was needed.

Hannah's excitement top notch though visibly exhausted, she packed the small bag with the used clothes and passed it on to Divine. Mwasa helped with helping the boy off the bed which obviously brought the boy discomfort at how roughly he was being manhandled. Martha burst into laughter at the boy's expression before offering help to the oldman.

Loraine struck a conversation with one of the security personnel whom she knew had a huge crush on her dear soul. She loved teasing the man senseless until he resembled a love struck teenager. Tomilola signed the forms in the doctor's office. She avoided Troy's gaze like a pandemic and bolted out the door before anything. Luckily the feeling was mutual. He had sensed her discomfort the moment she set foot into his cabin. How they had been close friends in the past. It's a pity how they were now strangers who knew each other.

He couldn't blame how awkward their meeting had been. The lines had been defined.

Unfortunately, he now had more questions than answers from the past. Roman shut the past off completely and said not a word about what had really split them. Now he worried that the past had returned and it was barely two weeks before he walked down the aisle to ask for Michelle's hand in marriage. If only he knew he had a son!

The escort left the hospital grounds. Jason and Hannah had become the best of friends as the woman was good at pampering. She had pleaded with Tomi to let him spend the rest of the week with the oldies. She could not find it in her to refuse her especially when her siblings cheered for her to say yes. That evening, she had found a notification from her bank that it had been credited with money. It had to be her father. He had been doing that from the time she left home. It would have been selfish of her to not allow Jason spend a few days with them.

She decided to treat Divine out that evening. He was indeed the brother she had always wanted. Bidding him to dress up, they hit the road to the center of the city.

Fists of fate

Fate loves the untold challenge. Sometimes you have to rencocile the past to move to the future. Divine understood this part of life so well when they took seats in the diner.

Cafesserie.

He had been deeply engrossed into the conversation he was having with Tomi that when the blow hit hard, it hard him tightening in pain. Sandra was in the same room with him. He had loved the woman from the age of ten but somehow fate had decided otherwise.

His brows creased. He felt hot. His palms and back drenched in sweat. His nostrils flared. At the change in countenance, Tomi followed his gaze. She was devastated at the wrong choice of venue. She swiftly asked him that they leave but he stubbornly inclined into his seat the more swearing halfheartedly how he was okay with the arrangement.
Tomi slumped back into her seat knowing there was a storm brewing somewhere in the abyss.

The kind waiter returned with their orders.

As she grabbed a napkin to start digging in, her senses heightened all of a sudden at the cologne that had wafted into her nostrils. Her cutlery dropped clattering on the floor drawing attention to their direction.

"Shit."

Divine mouthed. Her attention had been locked by someone else. He had turned at the clunking noise and then it happened. Her gaze entrappeyes had locked. Recognition stamped in and he swallowed a lump of saliva. She just couldn't look away no matter how hard she tried. Her stomach did summersaults. She could feel the hairs on her skin rising and then like a hurricane, she remembered his words, "You're nothing more than a friend to me."

That was enough to return her control. Drunk from his stare, her body shivered. She could still feel it boring into her back. Troy watched quietly without saying a word. This was the least of his expectation that he would see her again the same day. Excusing herself to the lavatory, she swayed graciously in black stiletto heels and red body con dress. It had accentuated the right places. Anyman would be up if he stared at her cat walking just a little more.

There wasn't a trace of motherhood in her. She was just the same damsel he had met in freshman year. Tomi released the breath she did not know had been locked down her throat. Her lips felt dry even with the gloss. Taking deep shallow breaths, she couldn't understand how he still affected her that much. Was it because she hadn't had anyone after him? Or was it the realization that she still felt something for him and still harbored the wish that one day he would be hers. Wishful thinking,

Several minutes she pep talked herself before saunting out the bathroom and being cornered in the hallway. They had bumped into each other and he cursed beneath his breath. She did what she knew best, went back into the ladies' wing and calculated for a few minutes before walking out. This time around, she settled the bill and dragged Divine out of that place. He noticed how badly it had affected her from how silent she was as they took the drive home in a taxi.

Troy netted Roman into telling him if at anyone point something had happened between the two of them in the past. Caught off guard, the latter had gulped down the glass of cocktail before shaking his head in refusal.He nearly choked from the way he was shoving down the food. The former did not push. He knew with time everything would finally be in the light.

Down his earlobe and further to his chest line. The traces of her fingertips sent spasms and electric shivers bolting down his spine. He yanked her up setting her on the island with her legs twined around his middle. The unending assaults on her lips and soft moans filled the kitchen.

Her hands went below his belt line as he arched. He took her lips again as the small peice of night cloth came off. The burning in their eyes as he-

Roman stirred from sleep hard and blue. She had now gotten into his sleep too. Damn that woman! He couldn't help cursing the wicked dream. She had taken him back to that night. Thier fisrt night as they made love. Just when he thought he had his past wrapped around his fingers, she returned to taunt his efforts. He found himself in the bathroom under cold water trying to calm himself down.

He had spent the night alone as Michelle had gone to see her parents about the official visiting of the man before the traditional marriage. He needed to get a grip on this lest it destroyed him. Grabbing his cellphone, he phoned Troy and asked him to come over. The last time he had decided to battle something like this alone, he had ended up in a down alley. A mistake he would never repeat as long as he was still sane.

A knock cmae through the door . He led him to the breakfast bar and offered him coffee before he actually told her that he was getting more frustrated with his thoughts. Tomilola was plunging him everytime his head hit the softness of the bed. Troy listened attentively before asking him again if something had happened between them in the past.
Too tired to negate, he confirmed with a positive nod. Torn between telling him that he had actually bedded her and how he knew that he had left her when she needed him the most.

The former not wantind to add salt to the wound, decided to keep his findings to himself.

Monday 11:00am, a brown parcel came in for Mr. Mwasa. The head of security handed it over after confirming to the boss that everything was inside. The old man walked briskly to his office and tore the paper impatiently scattering the contents on the table.

A photo of popped up first of a man and woman of the same age bracket. The woman probably twenty four around the same age as Tomi he mused while the man, Just a year older from the documentation.
His fists clenched with vessels almost purple at how happy they were, how his hand held down her waist. His eyes burned with fury. He was about to do something he was going to regret.

The dates couln't be more correct. Grabbing a faded envelope from the desk drawers at the right top, he passed on the bulging bundle to his officer before taking his seat again.

The striking resemblance couldn't be dismissed. He was his father's son indeed. His address and location were all detailed. It was easier that his mobile contact was there in plain blue print. Punching in the digits into his office desk phone, he waited before a few rings when the call connected.

Later that afternoon, Loraine and Martha in the company of their mother, had warned the headteacher about any bullying towards Jason. They had threatened that if it happened again, though a private school; they would have it shut down. The headteacher's office had been in chaos when they had asked her to summon the staff who had let the fight carry on between the children in class without intervening.

The women had been boiling like enraged dragons at the woman's refusal. Everything had gone out of hand when the director had been phoned. The man had arrived and had of the counts thhough a bit exaggerated about the fights. The storm had maddened when the mother of one of the pupil's who was fond of harrassing Tomilola had been invited to the school.

Andrew Mukasa the director had had to suspend the teacher to appease the woman and warn the other parent directly. When her wrath was satisfied, they waited till school time was done before Jason was picked from class. They had informed Divine earlier in the day. Most of the pupils had been mesmerized at the turn of events in favor of the boy. No one had expected him to have such a backing. There was more to Tomilola than the surface water. The bursar took one last glance at the receding vehicle, before walikng away.

Michelle returned home all smiles that her parents had finally agreed on a date she could bring her man down to their home. The door knob twisted of their apartment and she pulled in the suitcase. Sensing masculine cologne in the house, she smiled broadly wondering if Roman was in the house. She halted in her steps when she walked into a room filled with men clad in black suits. There was a man at the counter in her kitchen who was sipping tea.

He's face hardened as was his gaze.

"Go-- good eve, good evening gentle-men." She stuttered while trying to calm her nerves.

One of the men grabbed her bag and the other her suitcase rather gently before she could think about ringing someone and compromising their presence. The old man bid her to take a seat opposite him. He's kind gesture came off as rather rough and dainted with an ulterior motive. She had to be careful because she did not exactly know whom she was dealing with.

"Michelle Kwagala.?" He watched her expression as he said her name. He had wanted to meet the young lad but it had all worked into his favor when the woman instead had walked in. He preferred working with men. None the less,he could handle this.

"Yes please sir how can I help you." She had finally found her tongue.

" You know.Your boyfriend, Jonathan Roman owes me something. Has he ever told you about a woman named Tomilola?" The pain in his voice was evident.

"Probably not I guess. And may be if he did, they had to be bad things I assume. Otherwise how would you fall for him? Hmm."

Michelle's curiosity had immediately piqued the moment her name was said. She was the only person Roman had never told her about. She barely knew the woman. He had always brushed her off as the one disappointment he wished he never met. Her setting foot in his life had led him to depression. She was everything totally forbidden, dark, dangerous and even disastrous. He had described her as a friend would was pure venom.

Staring at the man in fron tof her, she knew there was something she might have missed from histroy.

"Now, this man of yours. Got Tomi pregnant and then just like that he left. She fell for his gentlemanly ways, she fell for his kisses, his touches, his everything. She bore him a son, his making seven on 10th. I can't believe she gave up everything for him; including family and then left her for you I guess."

His tone expressionless she listned as her confusion grew the more.

"It's a pity, that his not here. I just wanted to look him in the eye and ask why he would destroyed my daughter's life." The sound of breaking glass almost jolted her out of the seat.

"Now tell me. Do you think that reverend bishop father of yours and mother, what if they also disappear. Like boom."

He laughed so hysterically at the thought that Michelle's skin crawled. She could sense danger. She really loved Roman. But whatever this man had said about the boy, the other woman. He seemed so broken with his security. His face had caged wrath all over. If he had the power he would have wrecked everything around.

"When he returns, Send my regards. I will be in touch."

He stood up preparing to leave.

"Oh I almost forgot, I've been to Ladore countless times. You know Kawuki; be sure to greet me the people there."

From the creasing and worry drenching her, he knew she had understood that he had been meaning her parents.

The glow

Martha picked the call on the second ring as she walked to the laboratory for her first lecture. Loraine had called to inform her that she'd found a parcel with information about the supposed father of Jason. The two bickered for sometime as they discussed why their father would do to the young Lord. He had lond swore to break the lad's legs for messing up his daughter's life.
The plan had been plainly abortive when Tomi confirmed his worst nightmare. She had told everyone just how much she loved Roman that she was willing to jeopardize her family for him.

If love wasn't blind how could one end up like this? Her father had queried his desperate offspring. He was so disappointed that she was weak when it came to love. Not once had she ever used her head. All her decisions were based on how deeply she felt. He hated for a fact that someone had caught her highly unattained attention and them stamped everything in the mad.
 It was going to take long before she fully forgave herself for the choices she made because she couldn't see the better options she had at the time.

Surprisingly, she had retorted that he was the one person who walked into her life and taught her how to be happy and not fight all the time, to rest even when she was brave, to see the sun where she once saw the clouds. He had been the person who believed in her baby steps when her parents refuted her choices. He was kind to her when she needed it and that's all that mattered. She mistook his kindness for love, that was on her.

Mwasa exasperated at the nonsense his daughter was spewing, had raised his hand on her in fury causing a thunderous clap and blood to drip from her lips. With swollen lips, she had still maintained her stance and his heart twisted in agony. This was too much for him to bear. That night, Hannah had threatened to leave him in tears if he dared struck on their child again. The rest of the siblings had ran off to bed with the traumatic events that had happened that night.

Everyone had always insisted that love hurt. That was a false ideology to her. Rejection was a pain in the ass, loneliness was another thorn, envy ruined, losing someone brought pangs of sufferring. It was like people confused all this with love. Deep down, love was the only emotion in the universe that concealed the pain, it made her alive, ignited a burning so hot within her, When she found love, it was the only thing that enfolded her disappointment. That she found with the life in her belly.

Tomi had insisted on bearing everything for the sake of her unborn child and her unrequinted love for the man she could never have. Turns out he had actually stayed by her side out of pity and her constant tantrums to commit suicide. She now understood how she had selfishly kept

him by her side and buckled him up with emotional blackmail. Why did he have to burn her soul with emotional contentment when he couldn't offer it?
Why did he have to introduce her to loyalty, to happiness and take it away all of a sudden!

Her body had curled in a ball that night in the cold as she left home when she couldn't give up the baby. Physical pain wasn't the most painful after all. The wretching, nerve tearing that ate her up from the inside was enough to turn her up into an insane crack bug.

She couldn't imagine he had promised to forever stay by her side only for him to yank that away pitifully. Six years had played their part. She had taken training in the army. Her father wanted to teach her on how to follow orders. She had been taken on a mission just to see how cruel the world was. The political dirty game had been taught to her from childhood a rally she seemed to have forgotten.

When she had promised to not have contact with anyother man, he had finally taken her back to school with a lot of pressure from his wife and the two siblings.

An email notification popped on Divine's screen.

"Dear miss Tomilola Linda,
In response to the informaton sent ealier, you are now welcome to work with Knowle hospital with effect from tommorrow at 8:00am. The human resource will provide you with the financial details. Senior registered nurse Kolli Dombolo will provide you with a working schedule. See

you tommorrow.
Your's warmly,
Senior Reg Administrator,
Rachel Kasibante."

He read it aloud to a smiling Jason and a thrilled Tomi. She had not applied to Knowlw hospital. Nothing could jog her memory to link anything with that huge health care facility.

Divine volunteered to drive her to work the following morning after dropping Jason off at school. They had dinner together. The former helped with the home work while Tomi did the dishes. He later tucked him into bed.

"Uncle Divine." He tugged lightly on his sweat shirt.

"Who is my father? What his name? Will I ever see him? I'm I really that bad that he would not love me?" He interrupted the banter with a "hush child." Eyes moist, he massaged the temples to calm him down.

" I had grandpa tell mumshie that he had found the "bastard" who had got momma pregnant. I have been wanting to ask you since momma never answers any of my questions. She just avoids them. Is he really a bastard?"

Divine watched as he retold probably an adult conversation he had eavesdropped while with them painfully.

"Your father is a good man Jace. He loved your mother so much. That's why they made you. The reason why momma doesn't tell you these things is because you're her baby. Now go to sleep and don't peek into adult conversations again. Momma would be furious you know."

He promised to get him a photo of his father when he started pestering for a name. He had no choice but to tell the boy. Jason got out of the covers and encircled his tiny little hands around his neck. Warm liquid soaked the grey cotton and he caressed his back tenderly before he could succumb to sleep.
Tomi heard a little commotion from the room and walked in.

Fortunately for Divine, the boy was fast asleep.

Roman returned to a packing Michelle. She had set a suit case by the bedroom door. Holding the small handbag, she made for the door only to run into a hard chest. Tired from work, the sight confused him.

"Baby are we going on a trip alraedy?"

"Don't baby me Roman. Goddammit why didn't you tell me? Were you waiting for the right moment? Or you would never breathe a word. It hurts that you have to keep secrets from me you know! Why?"

"Hey, what's happening. Calm down baby we can talk about this."

He reached for her hand but she took a step backwards.

"I don't want to talk about this. You have a son for heavensake. A son with Tomilola."

Her voice cracked yet he was far from understanding what she meant.

"A son? Tomilola? What are you talking about?"

He reached for her yet again as she hit him countlessly. Nonetheless he held her so tightly until she quietened down. Pulling her into his laps, she recounted the events. His heart sunk to the depth of his stomach, Karma was surely a bitch. It had finally caught up with him. He made her cinammon tea and cuddled her to sleep.

When he was sure the snatchy forty winks had got to her, he carefully and stealthily got out of bed. He needed to sort this fast foward before it ruined his relationship. The call he had ignored earlier was probably the cause of what had happened.

Tomilola Linda! She was indeed the mistake of his life.

Divine seated in the two seater sofa reading celebrity scoop on his phone when a call came through on Tomi's mobile cell. It was a new number. He was never one to pick new numbers. This reaked of trouble. She asked him to pick the caller since she was still in the bathroom.

He maintained the silence until the caller from the other end said something.

"Hello." "Uehm hi.. Good evening. Tomi are you there?"

Divine would have known that voice from anywhere. Roman! The man had balls. It was such a good time to castrate and bisect the lad in bits but he needed to be civil. Worse still that she still had a soft spot for him.

He ended the call without a word when she walked out of the bathroom and asked him who the caller was. He innocently told her it was a wrong number and asked her to get some rest. Tomi knew when he was being weird. He always scratched his palm whenever he lied to her about something. She smiled wryly before picking her phone and into her bedroom.

An hour later, a call came through snatching her slumber. She was mad at the caller for ruining her night and still ended the call. Persistently, the buzzing of her mobile left her highly irritable that she lashed outrightly when the call connected.

"Didn't they teach you any manners not to call women at night abi. Who does that? If you try disturbing my sleep again i will block you. How can you stress me on my own phone?"

"Tomilola Linda."

The serenity in the voice calmed the storm in her. She held her breath and froze with eyes heavily dilated.

"Roman?"

Her voice barely a whisper.

"Tomi, good evening please. This is Roman. I'm sorry for calling this late and for how i acted recently. But i would like you to spare me sometime so we can talk. Tomorrow if you don't mind. I will text you the place and time. For the sake of old times."

The line was dead silent. Numerous questions roamed her mind. Where did he get her number from? He had not wanted to talk to her for six years why the sudden change of heart.

"Hello. Hello Tomilola."

" Roman i don't want to see you neither do i want to talk to you. For old times sake, leave me the hell alone. I've done a great job at keeping my distance so please, keep yours."

She could barely breathe by the time she finished rapping the words. Her heart twisted once more in pain and her eyes glistened. You never get used to pain. Not even time could lessen that feeling. She was so done with loving him and how his voice melted her walls down. She hated the fact that she missed him badly and couln't find it in herself to hate him completely. She had to always pick up the pieces of her frustrated attraction.

Love that ignites the soul

The human resource was kind enough to Tomilola when she reported to work by 7:30am. She signed the financial statement forms after her salary scale was endorsed, Three million for the start wasn't bad money. It was good for her age and not a lot of experience with the hospital setting.

The head nurse sister Dombolo handed her a file and a working rota on arrival to the wards. She was oriented around the theatre, labor suit and surgical ward where she would be rotating for the first month. Sister Margaret was assigned as her assistant until she could finally run a ward as an in charge on her own. The middle aged lady displeased that someone would be replacing her soon started plotting evilly on how to rid her from her territory.
An ambulance rushed in a couple of minutes later with am expecting mother who had experienced an obstructed labor and inadequate pelvic inlet. Sister Dombolo requested Tomilola to scrub and assist in the theater as the nurse on duty had not reported on duty.

The doctor was informed on the emergency development and later joined in the gowning as the circulation nurse prepared the instruments.

While fastening headcap, the doctor was warned to go easy on the nurse as she was new in the hospital. He fancied not the idea of newbies or working with them. The nurse was placing a fluid bag on the patient when he walked in to the operation table.

The drapes secured he requested for the surgical knife when that familiar pair of eyes met his. He was taken aback but swallowed the shock plastered on his face. The rest of the operation went smooth in deadly silence. It would have made the situation easier as she avoided him rather it startled him further. The recovery room nurse on the hand over from the theatre noticed how the doctor stole glances at Tomilola.

The woman was indeed a sight to behold. She looked like those women with dripping bodies from the waist. She couldn't help but admire how she carried herself while working.

"Sister Tomilola please join Dr. Roman for the ward round. I will be needing someone to check the supply log books of the post operative ward." The old matron indulged.

He was buying more time so he could inquire how ended up working at his place of work. Was this all her father's doing? She had refused his request yet somehow show up the next day where he operated his tasks, whom was kidding? He was past playing such mind games. She jotted down the clinical notes which he signed later in his office.

He requested the head nurse to send her in after her duty that afternoon.

She walked in after knocking softly and he shut the door roughly behind her.

"What are you doing here Tomi? Really? You show up at my work place and pretend you're the new incharge. Was this your genius plan all along?" He'd kept himself in check all the while at the operating table and that had flew away with the privacy of his room. She yanked his grip out of his hands when he caged her.

He could smell her perfume. Vanilla with a mixture of innocence. The redolence still a taint of red seduction and sensuality. Though faint, his nostrils would pick up that fragrance anywhere. Breathing it in released a series of combusting pheromeones. Damn.

The same old one!

"So you think you're the only one allowed to work in places like these? How arrogant! And if it brings you better sleep at night, my father got me this job. So be careful if you don't want this snake right here to suck the life out of you."

She venomously spat before pushing him with all her might.

"Tomi. The same old feisty woman. It's a pity you'll be fighting a losing game now that we have a son together. Don't you think." He smirked watching her squirm uncomfortably on her feet.

"We." Her fingers darted between them; "we don't have a son together. So don't you dare pull any stunts because I will wage war if I have to."

Her lips plump and ready for an assault but he looked away instead. He had loved upsetting her in the past because of how extremely provocative and sultry she presented her arguments with the bossy tone. The touch of an alpha was still intact. He found his gaze roaming her from hair to toe. The dark in her eye consuming the white. He could have pushed her a little to the wall just to get her wiled up.

"Hmm. So we don't have a son together yet your father threatened my fiancee yesterday? Oh come on. So now you're won't say a thing. I thought we were playing a game? I. I mean, look at you! I thought y--"

"My father? What a cheap stake? You must am too gullible to fall for this!"

"Yes your dad. The secretary of defence. Major General bla bla bla."

Her hands had balled into fists ready to strike. He was definitely enjoying the torture he was putting her in. Her dilated pupils and strained wrist veins. She counted backwards from ten until she regained composure.

"If this is the way you flirt Dr. Roman. Change the cards, it's boring for my taste."

"I'm going to be watching you closely like a hawk."

"Of course doctor Roman. Since we don't have a patient case to discuss, i gotta go."

Women with pretending! His fist connected with the wall drawing blood from his knuckles. He was losing his sanity.

"Tomilola. Is that you?"

"Wilson. Dr. Wilson?" She dried the tears that were forming and offered her hand in greeting.

"Are you working here with us now? It would be lovely to see more often."

"First day of work actually."

"How's Jace. I haven't seen him in two years now? How are his lungs?"

"Well he's grown. Big boy, eats a lot and well his lungs are getting better. I started him on the new drug therapy you recommened. Thank you so much. I actually felt frustrated when i was told you were transferred."

"So you want to say you missed me huh!"

They both burst into laughter at the lame joke. He promised to catch up later after work and they dispersed. Roman had listened in to the entire conversation. He placed a call through to Troy. He had actually done the

DNA test just in case. The call came through as he read the results that confirmed his fear. Jason was his son.

Somewhere in downtown Miami.

Michelle narrated to Claudia her best friend what had happened between him and her. Claudia surprized, asked her if she would stay knowing that there was someone from the past involved. If it was confirmed that Roman had a son, then she had to definitely be a step mother something she wasn't ready to do.
That same afternoon, she rung her parents and called off the traditional marriage until further notice.

 Later that evening, Troy asked Roman to meet him at the usual place where they had drinks. It was time! He handed over the envelope on arrival. The furrowing of his brows and how he had banged the table loudly.

Tomilola sauntered into her father's house completely disheveled. She neede to confront the situation before it got out of hand. The entire family was in the living room watching the news.It had just been reported that a student from the neighboring town had hang herself in the wee hours of the night.

"Dear Lord! Depression is on the rampage these days.My girls, please talk to us if anything is a miss so we can help in time." Hannah remarked.

The look on her face when she walked in, told Mwasa that she had got wind of what happened. He feigned ignorance when she greeted him grudgingly and refused to have dinner. Her mother coaxed her into telling her why she had a long face. She couldn't bring herself to saying anything. Roman had nearly succeeded in turning her into a time bomb.

Her patience for tolerating the man had thinned. She had made mistakes yes. She had lied to everyone. She had betrayed their trust. Mentally she had been so doddery as Troy and once upon a time described. Her whole life was on tenterhooks and she treaded on eggshells. Her friends had been glad to deprecate and slander her when the opportunity presented on a sylver platter. After that they had phoned her and "begged" her to return to college.

She was no harlequin not to understand that she had been in the wrong circle all along. It was a pity that her "best friend" had told her mother that she had always envied her so badly and now her score had been settled. There was a rear view was always smaller than the wind shield. Roman better be ready not to cross her this time around. She had picked her broken pieces from the ground one by one and glued them back to her hacked flesh.

She knew magnitude of the power she refrained from using. Hesitancy wasn't going to be part of her routine.

When she was calm enough, her father took her on a stroll to the kraal so they could talk. He owed her an apology. The moonless night was far from dull with the flow of the conversation. He was yet to acknowledge that she was now a grown woman who would make rational decisions. He just needed to support and guide her. He offered a bunny hug before instructing one of his many drivers to take her home.

Twisted

In the presence of an attorney, Roman took a seat opposite Tomilola. They would never come to a truce if it involved Jason. He wasn't ready for the term father. This was his flesh and blood still. He was going to stand by the promise he had made her.

************Six years ago**************.

They had spent the night watching movies and gossiping. It had stormed with droplets from early evening to late afternoon. Tomi had been so melancholic at the sudden revelation how a trusted friend of hers had planned to have her gang raped. Her eyes swollen from snovelling. she had sought out his help. He had been her night in shining armour. He had showed up.

She had been helping her friend out with an assignment when her phone started buzzing. Just looking at the number, her breathing had hitched.

That had been the night he had bundled her up in cuddle while caressing her as she recounted. He had held her to sleep. The same night, they had kissed. The weather had been perfect. The cold of the zephyr in distinction to the warmth of their bodies. It was everything to her. After him, there had been no one else as good as him.

The following night, he had told her they were friends with benefits. She had been mad at him for saying she was no more than a friend to him that she marvelled if her touches were that repellant. Were her kisses that bad? They did not have the extreme physical chemistry, yes. He had been a drug she couldn't get enough of. He was everything she desired.

Intellectually fit, a good listener and arrogant in a way that ticked her. She was a bad boy who treated her right. Loyal and honest, a little blunt most times. Penetrating stare that got under her skin and so protective of her that she loved that side of him to the bone. Most times they would read together and he would challenge her with a competitive spirit. He would even complete her sentences and would plant playful kisses every chance he got. The long night walks, the photos, the movies and cuddles. Roman! They had danced in the rain and told each other what they wanted in the future.
It was fault after all. She had been too stubborn to let in anyone at the time. So she fell from the high horse. He was the only man that burned her soul and left her yearning for something she couldn't have.

Sitting across him, reminded her that Jason had been a huge blessing in her life.

"Tomi. If I get you pregnant because we're fooling around, we will have that baby. That's my baby. Our baby! And we will have to make this work for our son."

She had felt better afterwards though she had told him he wasn't any good. He thought she had not loved the smooches when she walked away. She had not planned on surrendering her life to him. She knew whoever he chose to give his surname, would be a very lucky woman. The meeting proceeded smoothly and they agreed on shared custody.

He was supposed to pick Jason on Thursdays through Sunday. She planned on introducing the father-son pair that weekend. Not knowing how the boy would react, she braced herself for the most embarrasing questions.

She made an order for mango ice cream before excusing herself to the powder room. He had actually been shocked when she had agreed to come down to the cafe for this. He mused it must have been after he'd mentioned that he was bringing a lawyer along that her stance had waivered. She was too smart to let this drag on to court and have their son become a center piece of unwanted attention and questions.

He had to admit she had hardly lost the allure. The way the red fitting dress had clung tightly to her curves. Knee length with parallel five inch nail heels. Her shoulder length Brazillian hair had gracefully rested in patterns of waves. It was difficult to imagine that she had looked this enchanting just for the meeting. Knowing her well, she loved dressing this good. She had been the epitome of seduction and attention from the time she had rolled in.

Gazes of men flickered each time in her direction.

She cat walked taking her seat again before scooping a spoonful of the cold and moaning while the attorney gawked lustfully at her long ringed neck. What a shame that he had not earlier than this man who probably had issues with beautiful women. Tempted, Roman stealthily took a scoop when her eyes flickered open getting him right in the act. Her eyes narrowed meanly before a huge smile spread across her face when he dropped the act. She picked the same spoon and fed him.

Just like old times, this became a truce.

It was his turn to dish the sherbet when the spoon clattered on the floor. "What the he--?" Roman dumbstruck. Michelle so enraged.

A thunderous whack echoed. Tomilola could only caress her stinging cheek.

With her lips pursed animously, she emptied the glass of red wine into the former's hair earming her a lot of cheers. Michelle accused her of using emotional blackmail over her man to win him over like the desperate woman she was.

"I will not take shit from anyone Roman. The custody agreement is off. We would rather battle this in court."

"Oh now you have some morals lose woman?" Michelle mocked mimicking yet her accent.

"Both of you stop-!" Roman intervened only for the tables to turn; "And you honey, is this the emergency work you had to handle at the hospital? You lied to me because of this woman?"

Grabbing her bag, she stormed off to the counter and made payment. She had dealt with enough drama to deal with embarrassing show like this. She wasn't going to let some woman disrepect her just because of her past. That would call for a full fledged war. Roman angry at the turn out of events, gulped down the entire bottle of Light Haven red wine before he could face her.

Something about Michelle was changing daily and he failed to pin point what it was everytime he tried. He was breaking!

Epilogue

It was the eve of Jason's seventh date of birth.

Tomilola wrapped the jourrnal in a grey bag with red ribbons. She knew a time would come when her son would need answers. She dearly loved Roman! Such a bitter fact but true.

That time, this would be her safe guard.

Until then,she had to be strong.

Her heart weary and low, her phone vibrated while flashing. Dante.

Afterward

Detonate II is coming soon exclusively with more detailed content and drama.

Stay tuned for an update. Happy holidays!